Who cares for Postcolonial studies? The death of a literary movement.

TAPATI BHARADWAJ

Copyright © 2014 Tapati Bharadwaj

All rights reserved.

ISBN: 819287527X
ISBN-13: 978-8192875279

DEDICATION

...

CONTENTS

	Acknowledgments	i
1	Introduction	1
2	Locating the Self	11
3	Hybridity	18
4	The Death of Postcolonial Theory	26
5	Reading Gandhi and *Hind Swaraj*	32
6	Conclusion: The need to read primary texts	41

ACKNOWLEDGMENTS

The obsession with postcolonial theory has been with western discourses and a dominant theme is on how the Orient has been discursively represented by the West. Once upon a time, when the West was a global hegemonic power, we did care about these discourses as they represented us (read, the East) to the world and also to us. The task of postcolonial theory was to act like a conscience-keeper. But, these western texts are losing the sheen of power, and soon they will become historical artifacts, where we will learn how once-upon-a-time, the natives of the erstwhile colonized countries were perceived by the West.
Postcolonial theory, as a literary movement, is dying a gradual death.

1 INTRODUCTION

How catastrophic was colonial rule in India? In order to gauge the effects, we don't really have to go too far back in time, just a mere two hundred years or so, and it is just a pinch in time considering that we can trace back Indian history to 3000 BC. We can argue that the effects of colonial rule were so horrifying that it erased a civilization of its own history and culture, and instead imposed certain non-indigenous norms; moreover, the very economic and political basis of India underwent such devastating changes, that we still reel under its effects. The West got richer at the expense of the colonies, and the natives suffered. What is symptomatic of India can be representative of all the erstwhile colonies.

The question, then, would be: what exactly was erased when the Britishers arrived in India as colonial rulers? One clear example is the educational system that underwent numerous changes, and would one argue that the indigenous forms of education were superior to what was offered by the West? Were we natives really compliant in the civilizing mission and wanting to be a part of this civilizational change that was represented by the West? We rarely stop to think as to how it was for natives in precolonial India and whether they really wanted an epistemic shift. In the early years after British presence in India, that is between 1780 and 1830 or so, what was the nature of the educational practices that were introduced? With the advent of western education, were the natives psychologically scarred beyond recognition into becoming mutants, unrecognizable even to themselves. What is surprising is that all postcolonial scholars across the board rarely look at the life of Rammohun Roy (1772-1833) and his voluminous literary writings in English.[1] He was the first public intellectual in India, engaging with a global audience in English. His writings are extremely important as primary texts which document how elite natives looked upon the changes that were being introduced by the Britishers in the early years of colonization.[2]

What is of relevance here is that Rammohun was an intermediary of sorts, explaining the natives to the Britishers in the early decades of the nineteenth century, which meant that his own life has been carefully documented, as he himself made epistemic shifts. As a young man, Rammohun was educated in Bengali, and later Persian as the latter was the official language. We can speculate that his education would have been a model of how many young native, elite men in pre colonial India would have been educated. He was sent to Patna to learn Arabic, where he was taught from Arabic translations of Euclid and Aristotle, the Koran, and the writings of the Sufis. Subsequently, he studied Sanskrit at Benares. About this period he wrote:

> In conformity with the usage of my paternal race, and the wish of my father, I studied the Persian and Arabic languages, these being indispensable to those who attached themselves to the courts of the Mohamaden princes, and agreeably to the usage of my maternal relations, I devoted myself to the study

---

[1] A large part of this book has already been printed in *Rammohun Roy (1772-1833): a public intellectual and the arrival of native printed texts in India. Mastering imperial print: acts of resistance and collaboration* (Lies and Big Feet, 2014).

[2] Throughout this book, I will refer to Rammohun Roy as Rammohun. For his works, I have referred to: *The English Works of Raja Rammohun Roy. Parts I - V*. ed. Dr. Kalidas Nag and Debajyoti Burman (Calcutta: Sadharon Brahmo Samaj, 1948).

of the Sanskrit and the theological works written in it, which contain the body of Hindoo literature, law and religion.[3]

He studied in five different languages, namely, Sanskrit, Arabic, Persian, Urdu and Bengali. The Sanskrit and the Arabic systems of education were very different from each other, but each is seen as indispensable to the other. Rammohun reveals remarkable ease in how he was able to master these two varied systems of knowledge. If he was able to comprehend, simultaneously, two different epistemic systems, it is not surprising that subsequently he grasped the revolutionary characteristics of European, modern knowledge. By the early nineteenth century, Rammohun Roy became a great proponent for western education, negotiating between the Hindu-Islamic past and the westernized present.

But, this aspect of the colonial subject is rarely addressed. Who is the native, then, who haunts all dominant discourses of postcolonial theory? The image of the passive native is present in Gauri Viswanath's *Masks of Conquest*, when she writes that the discipline of English was part of the "imperial mission of educating and civilizing colonial subjects in the literature and thought of England, a mission that in the long run served to strengthen Western cultural hegemony in enormously complex ways."[4] According to her, "a great deal of strategic maneuvering went into the creation of a blueprint for social control in the guise of a humanistic program of enlightenment."[5] Infact, the introduction of English literature marks the "effacement of a sordid history of colonialist expropriation, material exploitation, and class and race oppression behind European world dominance" and the English literary text functioned as a

---

[3] Ibid., p. 461.

[4] Gauri Viswanathan, *Masks of Conquest. Literary Study and British Rule in India* (New Delhi: Oxford University Press, 1989), p. 2.

[5] Ibid., p. 10.

surrogate Englishman in his "highest and most perfect state" becoming a "mask for economic exploitation, so successfully camouflaging the material activities of the colonizer."[6] The native, in this instance, was a compliant subject, undergoing drastic cultural changes under British presence. More importantly, the implication is that all natives in India lived in absolute harmony in pre colonial times.

Before Macaulay's absolute diktat in 1835, there was no clear cut principle that the British government followed in its educational policies towards the Indians. The social history of the first two decades of the nineteenth century reveals contradictory ideologies; while the British government seemed keen to perpetuate the indigenous, traditional educational systems in Bengal, there were many Indians who were quite against it, the most vociferous being Rammohun Roy. In an address in Fort William, in 1811, Lord Minto summarized his plans for setting up Sanskrit Colleges in Tirhut and Nadia.[7] As science and literature were "in a progressive state of decay among the natives of India," his apprehension was that unless the "government interpose[d] with a fostering hand, the revival of letters" would "shortly become hopeless from a want of books or of persons capable of explaining them." Learning was the responsibility of the kings and in their decline, so had royal patronage towards education. Therefore, according to Lord Minto, the British government should not fail "to extend its fostering care to the literature of the Hindus and to aid in opening to the learned in Europe the repositories of that literature." Dissemination of

---

[6] Ibid., p. 20.

[7] "Appendix D. Lord Minto's Minute on Sanskrit College in Tirhut and Nuddea. Fort William. 6 March, 1811." *Selections from Unpublished Records of Government for the Years 1748-1767 inclusive. Relating mainly to the Social Condition of Bengal. Vol. 1*, ed. Rev. J. Long (Calcutta: Office of the Superintendent of Government Printing, 1869).

knowledge would enable the prevention of crime. Teachers and professors would be appointed, alongside librarians. A public library would be "attached to each of the colleges ... with a small establishment of servants for the care of manuscripts"; moreover, "ready access [would] be afforded to both the teachers and the students, and likewise to strangers ... for the purpose of consulting, transcribing the books, or making extracts from them."[8] These were indeed grand plans. The emphasis was on ensuring the continuation of Indian learning.

There was an equally strong native lobby that vouched for the introduction of Western education. In a letter to Lord Amherst, in 1823, Rammohun Roy, voiced his criticism towards the government in its decisions to open a Sanskrit College.[9] In fact, he hoped that the English government would devote the money for education and towards "employing European Gentlemen of talents and education to instruct the natives of India in Mathematical, Natural Philosophy, Chemistry, Anatomy and other useful sciences, which the Nations of Europe have carried to a degree of perfection."[10] To Rammohun, there was little merit in continuing with the indigenous system of education. A large amount of time was spent in learning the Sanskrit language, and the "learning concealed in [it?] under the almost impervious veil" was "far from sufficient to reward the labour of acquiring it"; if the aim was to promote the language of Sanskrit, he argued, it could be done so by granting allowances to the teachers.[11] It was of little use to encourage young men to spend the "most

---

[8] Ibid., pp. 554-560.

[9] "Letter of Rammohun Roy to Lord Amherst," in Sophia Dobson Collet's *The Life and Letters of Raja Rammohun Roy*, ed. Dilip Kumar Biswas and Prabhat Chandra Ganguli (Calcutta: Sadharon Brahmo Samaj, 1900). Reprint 1988.

[10] Ibid., p. 422.

[11] Ibid., p. 422.

valuable period of their lives in acquiring the niceties of the Byakarun or Sanskrit Grammar."[12] Moreover, improvement of the mind could not take place from studying the issues of the Vedanta: "In what manner is the soul absorbed into the deity? What relation does it bear to the divine essence?"[13] Central to native education was the study of Vedantic doctrines which Rammohun summarized as:

> all visible things have no real existence; that as father, brother, etc. have no actual entity, they consequently deserve no real affection, and therefore, the sooner we escape from them and leave the world the better. Again, no essential benefit can be derived by the student of the Meemangsa from knowing what it is that makes the killer of a goat sinless by pronouncing certain passages of the Veds.
>
> Again the student of the Nyaya Shastra cannot be said to have improved his mind after he has learned it into how many ideal classes the objects in the Universe are divided, and what speculative relation the soul bears to the body, the body to the soul, the eye to the ear, etc.[14]

Sanskrit education, in other words, would keep the country in "darkness." Education of this kind was dependent on rote learning, and manuscripts were used. In order to change the very nature of such a system and the fundamental underlying principles, the establishment of schools, and the dissemination of printed textbooks were essential. Eventually, colonial educational practices were

---

[12] Ibid., p. 423.

[13] Ibid., p. 423.

[14] Collet, *Raja Rammohun Roy*, p. 423.

successful as print made it possible for books to be disseminated.

The processes that accompanied colonization cannot be homogenized within the single rubric of economic-cultural-social oppression in the colonies. In this book, I argue that as a socio-cultural epistemic shift did take place, sometimes erasing the past or transforming it, it would be ridiculous to club this process as absolutely detrimental. It can be a very fruitful exercise if we looked at British colonization as being a multifaceted process: because this socio-epistemic shift did erase the past which might have needed to be transformed, but oftentimes the relationship between the colonizer and the colonized was one of master and ruler, Self and racialized Other.

Hindu pandits were impressed with the newness of western technology and the shift from a manuscript culture to a printed one seemed to have taken place quite effortlessly. Indian pandits attached to the Baptist Mission Press printed books of fiction in Bengali, and can thus be described as the first writers in Bengali who had their works printed. A few decades previously, this same group of pandits would have used manuscripts, but now were turning their efforts to print technology. *Pratapaditya Charita*, a biography of King Pratapaditya of Jessore, was published in July, 1801, and was written by Ramram Basu. Golaknath Sarma translated the Sanskrit *Hitopadesa* in 1802. *Batris Simhasan* was published by Mrityunjay Tarkalankar in the same year. 1802 also saw publication of Ramram Basu's *Lipimala, or the Bracelet of Writing*. In 1805, Chandicharan Munshi came out with a Bengali translation of the Persian *Tutinama*, titled *Tota Itihas*. Rajiblochan Mukhopadhyay published a biography of Raja Krishna Chandra of Nadia, *Maharaj Krshnachandra Rayasya Charitram* in the same year. The year 1808 saw Mrityunjay Vidyalankar publish two more books, namely *Rajabali*, a history of India till the British presence and a translation of the Sanskrit *Hitopadesa*. The Mission Press was, thus, also involved in printing books that were not meant for proselytisation.

Who cares how the West has conceptualized the natives?

What I have described above was one process of intellectual and technical exchange that allows us to understand the engagement between colonizer and colonized, English and native. Postcolonial theory can explain these engagements, and a lot of this theory operates from the premise that the colonialist, imperial project and its discourse inevitably and always makes use of specific fixed ideas to how the native "other" is to be defined: as "heathen, barbarian, chaos, violence".[15] For example, Homi Bhaba, in one of his seminal essays, "Signs Taken for Wonder," draws upon a narrative which describes natives being awe struck at the materiality of the printed book.[16] He also argues that the book as used by the natives was a hybrid formation; the "effect of colonial power," he writes, is the "production of hybridisation rather than the noisy command of colonialist authority or silent repression of native tradition."[17] In other words, Bhaba suggests that the engagement between the colonial powers and the native always results in a hybrid formation, which mostly becomes a derivative of the Original, and therefore, lesser in content. What exactly is this notion of the hybrid?

In this book, I closely look at how print, and the book, was transferred onto to India, and I have tried to understand the extent to which the dominant notions of postcolonial theory are relevant and valid, allowing me to understand the interaction between sly, barbaric

---

[15] Homi Bhabha, "Sly Civility," in *The Location of Culture* (New York: Routledge, 1994), Reprint 2005, pp. 132-144, p. 143.

[16] Homi Bhabha, "Signs Taken for Wonders: questions of ambivalence and authority under a tree outside Delhi, May 1817" in *The Location of Culture*, pp. 145-174.

[17] Ibid., p. 160.

native and the civilized colonizer. For the most, I conclude the book by arguing that the postcolonial notion of the hybrid is but pertinent in some instances, and has not been of much relevance in this context. I argue that the emergence of print technology in the colonial context and its subsequent usage cannot be contained within the notion of the hybrid; the complexities involved in describing the changes of a heterogeneous culture, that is in itself with porous borders, has to be seen on a continuum of change.

We do not have records or personal anecdotes of what it meant for a Brahmin in the late eighteenth and early nineteenth centuries to work and interact, socially or professionally, with the Britishers. Was this interaction fraught with a sense of racial otherness? It would be rather reductive to write off any relationship between the natives and the Englishmen as one that was between the white ruler and the ruled. In the pre-colonial past, many Brahmins had worked for the Muslim rulers without losing their caste; in fact, they had learnt Persian, which was the language of the court, and acquired Persianised social habits that were in conformity with the ruling class. In a similar vein, working for the British would not really have been socially difficult. The life of Rammohun and his forefathers who worked for the Muslim rulers explains how so many Hindus were able to interact with the British with relative ease. Social interaction of this kind made it possible for the easy transmission of European culture and knowledge into India.

Conclusion.

One can argue that the issue is this: to understand whether the natives were complicit and starry eyed at the newness of western civilization and not to agonize over the fact that western discourses that were written in the last two hundred years of global colonization were replete with images of the sly native [who is also a barbarian], versus the civilized West. Postcolonial theory has discussed, ad nauseam, the fractured psyche of the colonizer/colonized in the presence of the specter of the racial Other. The colonized were written over, and denied subjectivity. But all of this, at the present, is now passé. We have to keep in mind that simultaneously, during colonization, the natives were synthesizing two disparate cultures. As we historicize the emergence of postcolonial theory, it will allow us to declare the death of this particular theoretical and literary movement.

2 LOCATING THE NATIVE SELF

Locating the self.

We belong to a generation in urban India that really is unable to fathom the need to agonize about the foreign-ness of the West as we have normalized the presence of many aspects of western civilization in our lives; it is cool to speak English with a (south) Indian slightly incomprehensible drawl, eat with your fingers and be arrogant about the poverty that still exists alongside the overt wealth that it uber-evident all around. My parents were migrants to India from Bangladesh after 1947, and I grew up listening to many linguistic variations of Bengali; by the time my children grow up, the colonial past will be as distant to them as the Mohenjo-daro-Harappa civilizations. The colonial past for them will be another phase in the history of India, as was the Islamic past. Their generation of natives won't really care about how the Orient was discursively constructed by the West and that colonial-native relationships might have been fraught with tension and notions of power. Texts which deal with the white sahib, the civilizing mission of the white Europeans versus the effeminate, natives will be as anecdotal (and amusing) as cartoon strips. They will be so far removed from the memories of British-western colonization, that the past of the previous two hundred years will become, mostly, literary-textual sources for history. My children will say, "once upon a time, the West construed us within such racialized parameters of Other/barbarian and it is amusing for us as we read it."

The discipline of postcolonial theory is dying. The decades immediately after independence in India, that is post 1950s, meant the emergence of new nations that were formed from the erstwhile colonies. When natives traveled as non-western scholars and students to the supposedly centers of academic power in the West, they went with the identity of belonging to these once-colonies. It was not a bad identity; it was used in an empowering manner to point out accusing fingers at how heinously the West had been in its engagements with the colonies. Every aspect of the civilizational changes that had been introduced by the West onto the colonies was tinged with some shade of colonial authority and power. Texts were examined, alongside novels and fictional writings, to state the racist and oppressive nature of colonization.

It is not surprising that a large body of theoretical scholarship emerged, that examines the nature of western colonial encounters with the colonies. For the most, postcolonial theory has tended to focus on the engagement between Europe and the colonies they acquired in Asia and Africa. Frantz Fanon (1925-1961), for example, in his works arrives at a disenfranchised Alegrian identity which underwent absolute rupture in the presence of the French colonizer.[18] In *Black Skin, White Mask*, he writes that the black psyche undergoes alienation in the presence of the superior French culture. He describes the black man in the following manner:

> The black man has two dimensions. One with his fellows, the other with the white man. A Negro behaves differently with the white man and with another Negro. That this self division is a direct result of colonialist subjugation is beyond question.

---

[18] His following works are representative of his ideas: *Black Skin, White Mask*, Reprint of *Peau noire, masques blancs* (London: Pluto Press, 1986) and *The Wretched of the Earth*, Reprint of *Les damnes de la terre* (New York: Grove, 1968).

...

> Every colonized people – in other words, every people in whose soul an inferiority complex has been created by the death and burial of its local cultural originality – finds itself face to face with the language of the civilizing nation; that is, with the culture of the mother country. The colonized is elevated above his jungle status in proportion to his adoption of the mother country's cultural standards. He becomes whiter as he renounces his blackness, his jungle.[19]

For Fanon, European cultural engagement leads to a complete erasure of his black African identity. What we draw from Fanon, who was writing around the 1950s, is a notion of the hybrid where he describes a socio-psychical situation where the colonial subject was absolutely at the mercy of the colonial powers. This, though, cannot be representative and descriptive of all cultural encounters, as in many ways, it takes away all acts of agency from the perspective of the native. Such a Fanon-ian notion of the hybrid should not be definitive of how we describe cultural encounters and the inevitable give and take of languages, culture and technology.[20]

There has to be theoretical means which we make use of in order to describe cultural confrontations and engagements as did take

---

[19] "Remembering Fanon, Introduction," in *Black Skin, White Mask*, ed. Homi Bhabha, pp. 17-18.

[20] Postcolonial scholars, like Benita Parry, argue that valorizing ethnic identities allowed for oppressed cultures to survive the onslaught of imperialisms; citing the examples of Cesaire and Fanon, she writes that both "affirmed the invention of an insurgent, unified black self, acknowledged the revolutionary energies released by valorizing the cultures denigrated by colonialism." In Benita Parry, "Resistance Theory/ Theorizing Resistance or Two Cheers for Nativism" in *Contemporary Postcolonial Theory: A Reader*, ed. Padmini Mongia (London: Arnold, 1996), pp. 84-109.

place in the first few decades of colonial presence in Calcutta. Were the natives forever-always caught in the glare of the civilizing mission of the Europeans, forever denied a subjectivity as their histories were rewritten and they were remade to suit the needs of the colonial powers? Or were the natives complicit as they wanted change?

The need for binaries?

I draw upon examples from the Indian context as there is a plenitude of primary printed texts that were written during the last few hundreds of years, which documents the processes of colonization. The absolute binaries of civilized colonizer and unruly colonized undermines many documented events were written and this rhetoric is also dominant in most of the works that have emerged from the West during this time period. But this theme cannot be the overarching theoretical model which we use to describe the processes that accompanied the socio-cultural technological changes during the presence of the Britishers in India. Europe represented an epistemic shift from what India had been pre 1800s. In all probability, most native Hindus were star struck at the civilizational changes that were taking place and maintained a balance between two disparate cultures. For example, Rammohun Roy was a Sanskrit scholar, who was addressed as a *maulvi*, and also conformed to the prevalent notions of caste. He was also quite intimate with the ruling East India Cmpnay officials. Natives collaborated with the West as many aspects of modernity were transferred onto the colonies.

In a letter that Jeremy Bentham wrote to Rammohun Roy in 1831,[21] Bentham describes himself as having had a great influence on James Mill who dictated the histories of India through his work, *The*

---

[21] Letter from Jeremy Bentham to Rammohun Roy" in Sophia Dobson Collet, *The Life and Letters of Raja Rammohun Roy*, ed. Dilip Kumar Biswas and Prabhat Chandra Ganguli. (Calcutta: Sadharon Brahmo Samaj, 1900). Reprint 1988, pp.452-456.

History of British India (1818); Mill is seen as a family friend, a discipline and a student of Bentham. What is of immense interest is how Bentham subtly suggests to Rammohun that his ideas have been influential in determining the future of India, via the various people whom he knew (he mentions many officials of the EIC and James Mill, of course) and therefore, his establishment of the new penal system in England—the panopticon—is also an institution that Rammohun could consider for India. Bentham wrote, requesting Rammohun to join in the process of establishing an ideal prison system in India:

> What say you to the making singly or in conjunction with other enlightened philanthropists, an offer to Government for that purpose [of building the panopticon]? Professors of all religion might join the contract; and appropriate classification and separation for the persons under management provision correspondent to their several religions, and their respective castes; or other allocations under their respective religions.[22]

This is a fascinating anecdote to narrate, showing us the near macabre ways in which the new modern systems of knowledge that were emerging in the West were transferred to the colonies; Bentham suggests that the bodies of the native inmates would be classified and separated according to their religions and castes and a new panoptical system could be established in India. According to Michel Foucault, the panopticon's method of classifying and codifying was a perfect example of the new forms of knowledge systems that emerged in the eighteenth and nineteenth centuries where knowledge was intrinsically connected with power.[23] Foucault describes how the

---

[22] Ibid., p. 456.

[23] Michel Foucault, *Discipline and Punishment. The Birth of a Prison.* (New York:

eighteenth- to nineteenth-century transformation of the human sciences was "set in the context of practices of discipline, surveillance, and constraint, which made possible new kinds of knowledge of human beings even as they created new forms of social control."[24] The new systems of human sciences allowed for greater knowledge about the self, but simultaneously, made it inevitable that the body would be under greater control. State sponsored surveillance and discipline of the body produced "docile" bodies; as Foucault wrote:

> The human body was entering a machinery of power that explores it, breaks it down and rearranges it. . . . It defined how one may have a hold over others' bodies, not only so that they may do what one wishes, but so that they may operate as one wishes, with the techniques, the speed and the efficiency that one determines. Thus discipline produces subjected and practiced bodies, "docile" bodies.[25]

Bentham's prison system was one such institution which, through its method of control and surveillance of the inmates, was meant to create reformed bodies. The letter that Bentham wrote to Rammohun indicates that the structural changes that were taking place in the eighteenth and the nineteenth centuries, were in the process of being transferred to the colonies.

Vintage, 1995). Also see Michel Foucault, *The History of Sexuality, Vol. I* .(New York: Vintage, 1990).

[24] Joseph Rouse, "Power and Knowledge," in *The Cambridge Companion to Foucault*, ed. Gary Gutting (Cambridge: Cambridge University Press, 2006), pp. 95-122.

[25] Michel Foucault, *Discipline and Punishment*, p. 138.

The natives were at the receiving end of many of the new-fangled socio-technological discoveries and innovations that were taking place in the West. How did the natives engage with these changes? Even as we declare the decline of postcolonial theory as a literary movement, we can shift our focus onto the natives and how they transformed the western systems that were being imported to suit their needs. Doing so will allow us to make a theoretical move that will allow us a more nuanced understanding of the last two hundred years. Behind the façade of the servile native, the natives were synthesizing two disparate civilizations.

3 HYBRIDITY

Despite the whine and moan of all postcolonial theorists about the imperialist, civilizing mission of British rule in India, or in Africa, we really do not hear these scholars glorify the pre-colonial past. In order to declare the death of postcolonial theory as a literary movement, we have to consider ways to address the interaction between the colonizers and the colonized within an interpretative framework that is outside the binaries of Self-Other and civilized-barbaric. Because the natives were participants in the process, we also have to consider ways to address them outside the rhetoric of servile mimic men, despite the fact that most dominant accounts from the Center, both fictional and official, refer to them as such. More importantly, we have to understand that in the last two hundred years, the discursive portrayal of the East/ Orient (and the colonies) in most western discourses has been laden with recurring images of the sly, unreliable, pre-modern native. The issue is this: the natives did not really have much of a choice in determining how they were represented, because the colonial powers were not only their rulers but also global military powers. Postcolonial theory that has emerged in the academia has been the conscience keeper of western literature and discourses. But, the larger question in the present moment is this: these portrayals have become passé, as colonization in itself as a historical process has become an event of the past, and therefore, the cutting-edge nature of postcolonial theory has faded. It would serve our purpose better if we devoted our time to looking at how natives engaged with the new-ness of many aspects of western civilization in the last two hundred years. The onslaught of modernity in the colonies was not necessarily skewered.

An exemplary instance of how Indian society in the early years of British colonization engaged with the techno-cultural newness of the West is evident in Rammohun's involvement in the realm of print culture in Calcutta in its incipient stage. He knew the power of the printed text, and its capacity to travel across to unknown places and people. Even if we do not consider his Bengali writings, his English writings reveal an amazing degree of fluency with the nature of print culture. The readership of his English works was a large one, spread across different groups of people all across the English-speaking world. This characteristic of being aware of how to engage with different readers is what makes him unique. He was very conscious of his readership, and aware of what was needed from him as a native writer, writing for natives and for Europeans. For example, *The Precepts of Jesus, the Guide to Peace and Happiness; extracted from the Books of the New Testament ascribed to the four Evangelists. With translations into Sanskrit and Bengali*[26] was published in Calcutta in 1820. The irony was and is not lost. Here was a Hindu native, writing exegetical commentaries on the Bible. The readership would have undoubtedly been the European missionaries residing in and around Calcutta. In 1821, it was reprinted in America. Many of Rammohun's works that

---

[26] Raja Rammohun Roy. *The Precepts of Jesus, the Guide to Peace and Happiness; extracted from the Books of the New Testament ascribed to the four Evangelists. With translations into Sanskrit and Bengali.* (Calcutta, 1820). Reprinted in *The English Works of Raja Rammohun Roy. Parts I-V*, ed. Dr. Kalidas Nag and Debajyoti Burman (Calcutta: Sadharon Brahmo Samaj, 1948).

pp. 3-54.

were published from Calcutta were reprinted in England and in America. In a letter that he wrote to a gentleman in Baltimore from Calcutta, in 1822, the note of sarcasm is obvious as he describes himself as a defender of Christianity, and the missionaries as practicing heathen doctrines:

> I have now every reason to hope that the truths of Christianity will not be much longer kept hidden under the veil of heathen doctrines and practices, gradually introduced among the followers of Christ since many lovers of truth are zealously engaged in rendering the religion of Jesus clear from corruption.
>
> I admire the zeal of the Missionaries sent to this country, but disapprove of the means they have adopted. In the performance of their duty, they always begin with such obscure doctrines as are calculated to excite ridicule instead of respect, towards the religion which they wish to promulgate. The accompanying pamphlets called *The Brahmunical Magazine* and published by a Brahmun, are a proof of my assertion. The last number of this publication has remained unanswered for twelve months.[27]

Fundamental to our understanding of how English print operated in the early years of the nineteenth century is the fact that print shapes social relations. Rammohun was quite central in this process of Indians using print to engage with and against the newly established realm of the Britishers.

Social revolutions are dependent on print. The French

---

[27] "Letter," Calcutta; Oct. 27, 1822. In *The English Works of Raja Rammohun Roy. Part IV*, pp. 85-86.

Revolution, as Robert Darnton points out, was a result of the printing press—without the press, a group of men could "conquer the Bastille" but they could not "overthrow the Old Regime."[28] Printed texts, in the form of journals, almanacs, pamphlets, posters, pictures moulded the imagination of twenty six million French people during the Revolution. Drawing attention to the potential of the printing press, Robert Darnton wrote that the French "revolutionaries knew what they were doing when they carried printing presses in their civic processions and when they set aside one day in the revolutionary calendar for the celebration of public opinion."[29] Without print culture, runs Darnton's central argument, the French Revolution of 1789 would not have been possible.

Socio-political relations were redefined in the early years of the nineteenth century and print was intrinsic to these transformations. The specific focus here is on the English writings of Rammohun, and how he used print to engage with different groups of readers. We get a glimpse of the nature of different kinds of readership. The realm of native socio-religious intellectualism in the first few years of the nineteenth century in Calcutta was going through a phase of transition. This change is made clear if we look at the life of Rammohun; in his early years, he was well versed in Persian and Islamic theology. Subsequently, with the gradual political rise of the East India Company, the politics of the dominant Islamic past changed. As Hinduism became of immense interest to the Christian missionaries and Orientalist scholars, Rammohun thought it essential to engage with Hindu theology to combat their Westernised interpretations. The native Hindu intellectual community comprised both learned pandits and *babu* scholars. There were many Sanskrit pandits at that time, more learned than Rammohun. The list of *pandits*

---

[28] Robert Darton, *The Kiss of Lamourette. Reflections in Cultural History* (New York: Norton, 1990), p. xiii.

[29] Ibid., pp. xiii-xiv.

attached to the College of Fort William (1801) reveals the names of some of the existing scholars: the chief pandit was Mrityunjay Tarkalankar, the second pandit was Ramnath Vachaspati. Mrityunjay Tarkalankar was the finest scholar of Sanskrit in Bengal. Similarly, there were many rich, educated Bengalis, like Radhakanta Deb, who were patrons of knowledge. All of them were involved in print, writing polemical tracts. Rammohun inhabited such a realm of print, which involved both natives and Europeans. The different groups of people that Rammohun was addressing can be categorized in the following manner: native intelligentsia/ pandits, rich babus, non native intelligentsia, missionaries, East India company administrators and religious ministers in England and America. Thus, by mastering the conventions of print and by learning English he was able to address the Britishers on an equal footing. In fact, his English works were meant for a non native readership, to the point where he homogenized Hinduism and defined it as it was perceived by the Britishers and the Orientalist scholars.

The Vedantic texts in print.

Rammohun's Vedantic works can be described as the first Vedantic commentaries in a vernacular that were written for a non-Hindu, non-Sanskrit speaking readership.[30] He was aware of this as draws attention to this fact in *A Defence of Hindoo Theism*, "I must remark, however, that there is no translation of the Vedas into any of the modern languages of Hindoostan with which I am acquainted."[31] His works are exegeses on the commentaries of Shankaracharya and have a precedence in Baladeva Bidyabhusan's *Govindabhasya* and *Isabhasya*, which were the first Bengali commentaries that were written in the

---

[30] For more see Bruce Carlisle Robertson, *Raja Rammohun Roy The Father of Modern India* (Delhi: Oxford University Press, 1999), pp. 30-31.

[31] *A Defence of Hindoo Theism. In Reply to the Attack of an Advocate for Idolatory in Madras. 1817.* In *The English Works of Raja Rammohun Roy. Part II*, p. 85.

eighteenth century. The only exception was Dara Shukoh's translations two hundred years ago around 1641. Dara Shukoh was the oldest son of Jahangir, and attracted a liberal courtly crowd of scholars, imperial officers and nobles who followed the eclectic ideology of Akbar. He was a follower of Mullah Mir (d. 1635) and Mullah Shah Badeshi (d. 1661), two important Sufi teachers. He was firmly convinced that the Upanishads preached monotheism, in a similar fashion as did Islam. With the help of Brahmin scholars whom he invited from Benares, he translated fifty two Upanishads and titled the work *Sirr-i-Akbar*. In 1671, a French traveler to India named Francis Bernier returned to France with a copy of the Persian *Upanishads*, which were translated into Latin by Duperron and titled *Oupnek'hat*. It is not clear if William Jones knew this work when he, with his group of Benares *pandits*, translated the *Isa Upanishads* in 1799. He was assisted in his works by Hindu *pandits*, but none of their names are featured in the published works. In the early years of the nineteenth century, Rammohun, as a result of his familiarity with the officials of the East India Company and the Baptist missionaries, would have known about the works of William Jones and his collaborative use of pandits.[32] The reading domain within which Rammohun worked was already inhabited by European Orientalist scholars. It is almost as if Rammohun was challenging these scholars and their lack of acknowledgement of native support. His readers were the same as those of the Orientalist scholars. Here was an instance of a *pandit* who had turned Orientalist scholar.

Rammohun had a Western readership that was denied to all natives at that time. Native pandits were not referred to by the Western world. As a writer, Rammohun was able to imagine the needs of his readers, and adroitly negotiate between his English readers and his native readers. Rammohun had a readership that was immense in its diversity for that time period. His books found their

---

[32] See Robertson's *Raja Rammohun Ray* for more on this; pp. 10-54.

way into the hands of Jeremy Bentham, who, in a letter described him as "Intensely Admired and Dearly Beloved Collaborator in the Service of Mankind."[33] The *Precepts of Jesus* found its way to England, and it inspired the Earl of Northbrook to publish his *The Teachings of Jesus Christ in His Own Words*.[34] In the preface, the Earl wrote: "My purpose has been to put before them [the People of India] the Teaching of Christ in His Own words, as recorded in the four Gospels ... The learned and distinguished Hindu, Raja Rammohun Roy, published eighty years ago a compilation called *The Precepts of Jesus*.[35]

Printed tracts and pamphlets and newspapers became a medium through which Rammohun engaged with the socio-religious changes that were taking place. In particular, Rammohun was able to negotiate against the bullying tactics of many of the missionaries and conservative Christians who seemed to have found their way to India. Rammohun categorized the manner in which proselytisation took place: books were published and distributed amongst the natives reviling the Hindu gods; the second method involved "standing in front of the doors of the natives or in the public roads" to preach the greatness of Christianity and the "debasedness" of the others; and the third was to convert low caste people and hold them as examples for other natives to follow.[36] This exchange of religious opinion was not a passive exercise, whereby the missionaries coerced the natives to accept Christianity, but in fact, involved a great deal of humouring

---

[33] "Letter by Jeremy Bentham to Rammohun Roy," in Collet, *Life and Letters*, pp. 452.

[34] Earl of Northbrook, *The Teachings of Jesus Christ in His Own Words* (London: Sampson Low, Marston, 1990).

[35] Ibid., p. v.

[36] "Preface to the First Edition" of *The Brahmunical Magazine*, Calcutta, 1821. In *The English Works of Raja Rammohun Roy. Part II*, p. 137.

and satirising on the part of the natives. When Rammohun's *Precepts of Jesus* received enormous negative commentaries from an English reader, Dr Tytler in the *Bengal Harkaru*, who was a surgeon in the East India Company, and also a member of the Asiatic Society, Rammohun retaliated in the form of letters by assuming the name of Ram Doss, an orthodox Hindu and an opponent of all tenets of Unitarianism. Ram Doss pretended to be an enemy of Rammohun. This correspondence was published in a pamphlet titled: "A Vindication of the Incarnation of Deity as the common basis of Hinduism and Christianity against the schismatic Attacks of R. Tytler"[37] by Rammohun himself. The supposedly civilizing gaze of the Britishers was mocked by Rammohun, who could through his command of English and print, turn around the very means that were used to critique him.

In this chapter, I have examined the nature of the readership of Rammohun's English works, and how it became possible for him to pick up the socio-cultural processes of print culture. The Europeans settled in India and introduced certain institutions and systems of rule and governance, both for themselves and for the natives. The realm of print was one such institution. Gradually, the Indians learnt it, and replicated all aspects of print. This process of cultural transmission and exchange did not pass through any phase of mimicry.

---

[37] "A Vindication of the Incarnation of Deity as the common basis of Hinduism and Christianity against the schismatic Attacks of R. Tytler." In *The English Works of Raja Rammohun Roy. Part IV*, pp. 56-74.

4 THE DEATH OF POSTCOLONIAL THEORY

At the turn of the century, books made their way into Indian society and began to displace a manuscript culture. Natives started to read, make use of and negotiate their lives through printed texts. Moreover, the press initiated a shift in the very nature of how texts were to be written, preserved and disseminated. In fact, it initiated a shift in the very method of writing, a shift that involved cultural habits – Indians would sit on the floor and write, unlike Europeans who used tables and chairs. Nathaniel Halhed describes it in the following manner: "As they have neither chairs nor tables, their posture in writing is very different from ours: they sit upon their heels, or sometimes upon their hams, while their left hand held open serves as a desk whereon to lay the paper on which they write, which is kept in its place by the thumb: so that they never write on a large sheet of paper without folding it down to a very small surface"[38] It is fascinating to conjecture as to how exactly the change to print took place. As more and more natives had access to printed texts, that which had been the privilege of a particular class of people, now became democratized. Now, a large canvas of Indian society had access to printed books. How did it feel to be able to touch printed paper and read, and be aware that many others across the land were also reading the same text? Indians closely interacted with the Britishers and learnt their social manners, learning how the

---

[38] Nathaniel Halhed, *A Grammar of the Bengal Language*, 1778. Reprint, ed. R. C. Alston (England: The Scolar Press, 1969), p. 2.

technology worked. They also learnt the different uses that print could come into.

My focus is on a specific moment in time when the Britishers arrived in India; but before the Britishers came, India had always forever constantly negotiated with a vast array of cultural and religious invaders. Pre colonial India was influenced by Islamic culture. Indian culture that emerged under the Mughals would also have been hybrid, in the same manner as it was under the Britishers. So, what exactly is hybridity? Is it a cultural phenomenon, specific to the last few centuries. Helen Tiffin[39] makes such an assumption when she states that postcolonial cultures are "inevitably hybridized, involving a dialectical relationship between European ontology and epistemology and the impulse to create or recreate independent local identity."[40] She goes on to write that decolonization "invokes an ongoing dialectic between hegemonist centrist systems and peripheral subversion of them; between European or British discourses and their post-colonial dis/mantling."[41] Therefore, the project of post-colonial writings is to investigate the means by "which Europe imposed and maintained its codes on the colonial domination of so much of the rest of the world."[42] Tiffin assumes that native cultures were completely overwritten by colonial presence, and that Europeans dictated terms which left little space for natives to maneuver their positions and identities. The colonial culture,

---

[39] Helen Tiffin, "Postcolonial Literatures and Counter Cultures," in *The Post-colonial Studies Reader*, ed. Bill Ashcroft, Gareth Griffiths and Helen Tiffin (London: Routledge, 1995), pp. 95-98.

[40] Ibid., p. 95.

[41] Ibid., p. 95.

[42] Ibid., p. 95.

therefore, that emerged was hybrid but dominated by the superior European culture.

But this notion of hybridity that emerges only post colonization would not really be of much use in the context of cultures like India where pre colonial India was equally hybrid under Islamic rule. Tracing how the term hybrid has been used within postcolonial theory allows us to gain an understanding of how contentious and challenging a notion it is. Hybrid as a term has been co-opted by postcolonial scholars, across the board. Aijaz Ahmad points out that the term has become a "transhistorical thing, always present and always in process of dissolution in one part of the world or another, so that everyone gets the privilege, ... of being colonizer, colonized and postcolonial - sometimes all at once, in the case of Australia."[43] He writes, in his critique of the hybrid as has been used by postcolonialists:

> The idea of hybridity - which presents itself as a critique of essentialism, partakes of a carnivalesque collapse and play of identities, ... The basic idea that informs the notion of cultural hybridity is in itself simple enough, namely that the traffic among modern cultures is now so brisk that one can hardly speak of discrete national cultures that are not fundamentally transformed by that traffic.[44]

Ahmad's harsh criticism of theory that states that there does not exist "discrete national cultures" is antithetical to what is proposed by Homi Bhabha, who writes in his introduction to *Nation and Narration* that the boundary of national culture is "Janus-faced and the problem of outside/inside must always itself be a process of hybridity,

---

[43] Ajaz Ahmad, "The Politics of Literary Postcoloniality," in *Contemporary Postcolonial Theory: A Reader*, pp. 276-293.

[44] Ibid., 286.

incorporating new 'people' in relation to the body politic, generating other sites of meaning and, inevitably, in the political process...."[45] For Bhabha, hybridity is a colonial product, often erasing the agency of the colonized; for him, postcolonial criticism therefore, bears witness to the "unequal and uneven forces of cultural representation" in the contest for socio-political authority in the modern world order.[46] I would, on the other hand, pose the question whether all cultural engagements that have taken place between the natives and the Britishers have been unequal, in the manner as has been described by Bhabha. It is not inevitable, as I am arguing here, that the initial moments of contact between the natives and the Britishers was an unequal one; the colonizers would have introduced new systems of culture and technology, but the natives did not use them passively or in ways that were mere acts of Fanon-ian mimicry. The new culture that emerged was hybrid but in ways that showed the natives involved as active agents, deciding how print technology was to be used.

Here, I argue for a more nuanced notion of hybridity, one which would consider the process of cultural exchange as an ongoing one. It is not that colonial India gave rise to a hybrid notion of identity; Indian culture had always been in a state of being influenced by other cultures and colonial presence was but one more to the many other non-native, foreign presences. Infact, pre 1850s was a time period when the colonial powers had not become the monolithic institution that it later became, and there was more parity in the relationship between colonizer and colonized. For example, the early years of colonization had seen Warren Hastings' emphasis on Orientalist learning and this eventually gave way to a more interventionist

---

[45] Homi Bhabha, "Introduction" to *Nation and Narration* (London: Routledge, 1990), p.3.

[46] Homi Bhabha, The Postcolonial and the Postmodern, The question of agency," in *The Location of Culture* (London: Routledge, 1994), pp. 245-282, p. 244.

attitude of Charles Grant who wanted a more homogeneous India. Grant was elected to the board of the East India Company in 1794 and to Parliament in 1802 and it was because of his espousal of evangelical ideas of the Clapham sect that the East India Company introduced a pious clause into its charter of 1813. Post 1850s, with Darwin's *On the Origin of the Species* (1859) proposing evolutionary biology as a model of existence, Christianity was no longer a tool that could be used to control the natives and instead, imperialism was used as a religion to control the natives; print became an instrument of the empire.

My scholarship does not solely depend on an Eisensteinian, deterministic model, where print is seen as having an ontological status, prior to culture and affecting all aspects of society. The processes of colonization did affect what books were to be printed, and the use of the English language. The printing press had been introduced in India a long time ago; the Jesuits brought the technology in 1556, but its use was very limited. It was only with the advent of the Britishers, and with the import of printing presses, typesetters and editors from England, that printed texts were printed for large groups of people. This is a significant moment in the history of print in India. Therefore, when Nathaniel Halhed printed his book, *A Grammar of the Bengal Language* in 1778, he was codifying a local, regional language and giving it status by placing it in front of an English readership. That Halhed, who studied in Oxford and had literary ambitions as is evident in that he was familiar with Richard Sheridan, would travel to Calcutta as a writer of the East India Company and bring out a book on Bengali grammar is a fascinating anecdote, and represents the close interaction between England and India. The technology that he used in Calcutta was meant to be used so that printed texts could be distributed for a mass readership. The readers were Englishmen situated in England and in India, and the book was a first in its history. Within a few years, natives would also make use of print technology, and printed books would flood India, catering to the needs of the natives. This is a significant moment in the history of print in India. The book was a hybrid result, but how do we describe, or even theorize this notion of the hybrid? I have explained above that existing postcolonial theories of the hybrid fall short and it cannot be a valid theoretical tool in this instance. Hybridity can refer to the cultural exchange which took place and allowed the natives more agency in determining how to make use of the new technology/ culture that was flooding India.

5 READING GANDHI AND *HIND SWARAJ*

By the early twentieth century, which is when Mahatma Gandhi was writing *Hind Swaraj*[47] (1909), it becomes possible to gauge how ideas assimilated in his mind. In this canonical book, Gandhi synthesized two different world views, though often enough than not, he apparently rejected all things western. If we read through a text like *Hind Swaraj*, we realize how it performs a delicate balancing act. For arguments sake, which need not necessarily have a conclusion, if we pinpoint the start of British colonization in India at 1780, then we can state that it took only 130 years for a perfect blend of two disparate cultures to emerge.

Postcolonial theory has been obsessed in either engaging with how the Orient has been portrayed within stereotypical parameters in most western texts, fictional or otherwise, or in trying to analyze how western modernity was misappropriated in the colonial context and how it failed in most respects. One of course assumes that all was well before Western colonization. We refuse to accept that maybe, the synthesis that took place was good. It is within this interpretative framework that I read Gandhi's *Hind Swaraj*, where the writer arrives at a model for the Indian socio-political structure that has indigenous pre-colonial roots, while rejecting everything western. Despite the

---

[47] Mahatma Gandhi, *Hind Swaraj and Other Writing*, ed. Anthony Parel (Cambridge: Cambridge University Press, 1997).

vehemence against the West, which is obviously sheer rhetorical, the fact is that the underbelly of the book is based on an astute knowledge of how the West functions.

Reading Hind Swaraj.

As late as 1945, thirty six years after *Hind Swaraj*[48] had been written in Gujrati, Mahatma Gandhi was convinced – as is evident in a letter that he wrote to Jawaharlal Nehru -- that the Congress Working Committee would, in its considerations of how India as a free nation was to be, implement his ideology of a society that would emerge from within its own traditions rather than necessarily incorporate all the remnants of the British institutions. For Gandhi, in order to conceptualize the warp and woof of Indian society, one had to begin at the micro village level. "Truth and non-violence," he wrote in *Hind Swaraj*, could be realized "only in the simplicity of village life."[49] Agreeing that his ideal notion of the village was still in his mind, he wrote:

> After all every man lives in the world of his dreams. My ideal village will contain intelligent human beings. They will not live in dirt and darkness as animals. Men and women will be free and able to hold their own against any one in the world.[50]

Nehru's reply contained a strongly worded critique of Gandhi's position; not only did he find it difficult to understand as to why a village would embody "truth and non-violence" but he also made it clear that a village was not a repository of the qualities that were

---

[48] This is a canonical Gandhian text which contains the basis of Gandhian principles.

[49] Ibid., p. 150.

[50] Ibid., pp. 150-151.

being presented by Gandhi.⁵¹ Moreover, in Nehru's vision of Indian society, modern institutions -- like transport, a scientific community and research, presence of a well armed army – were essential if India was not to remain isolated. In order to grasp the full implication of this apparent ideological difference between Nehru and Gandhi – seemingly at loggerheads with each other – it would be appropriate to consider Gandhi's anti modernist attitudes as not only symptomatic of colonial resistance, but also view Gandhi as a member of a larger group of intellectuals and artists who were involved in critiquing the industrialization of modernity. It is easy to blithely categorize such anti-modern tendencies as a natural phenomenon of postcolonial conditions, but to indulge in such a view would be a rather simplistic endeavor⁵² for the appendix to *Hind Swaraj* reveals Gandhi's indebtedness to writers like Leo Tolstoy and Ruskin, amongst others, who were quite antithetical to the industrialization of Europe.

A refusal to engage with the changing conditions of the late nineteenth and early twentieth centuries was also symptomatic of numerous intellectuals and scholars of the modern period in Europe – Thomas Mann, Julien Benda, Krl Mannheim, F R Leavis, T S Eliot; as "kulturkritiks," Francis Mulhern writes in *Culture/Metaculture*, they were engaged in a "negative discourse on the emerging symbolic universe of capitalism, democracy and enlightenment."⁵³ For the practitioner of Kultukriticism, the "future of culture" was at stake in the moments of modernity and the main opposition was in the

---

⁵¹ Ibid., p. 152.

⁵² Gandhi distinguished between western civilization and modernity, considering modernity as an affliction of certain societies round the world, and not necessarily of western civilization *per se*. When referring to modernity and Japan as a nation, he writes, "it is the British flag which is waving in Japan, and not the Japanese" – implying that the Japanese achieved modernity by following the British example (41).

⁵³ Francis Mulhern, *Culture/ Metaculture* (London: Routledge, 2000), p. xv.

masses[54] and the only way to negate this was to recall back a notion of [elitist] tradition.[55] It would be erroneous to position Gandhi alongside this continuum, as Gandhi's critique, though of modernity, was based on ensuring that pre-British institutions of the state would emerge as dominant models and due importance would be given to village life. The nature of Gandhi's critique of modernity is central to my reading of *Hind Swaraj*.

For most scholars, what is not debatable is the fact that the processes of modernization accompanied British presence in India, but what is often quibbled over is how to account for its supposed failure. Sudipta Kaviraj argues that the experience of modernity in India did not simply imitate the West; by looking at certain aspects of the political in India – how the state, the nation and its institutions of democracy were established and imagined -- he questions that if modernity "shows a diversifying and pluralizing tendency in Europe itself," how would it be possible for different "cultures and historical circumstances [to] produce obediently uniform historical results?"[56] The very moments in history within which we locate Gandhi had seen and also saw constant transformations of the public and private spheres in India – at the behest of both Indians and Britishers -- and this has to be kept in mind when considering the extreme anti-modern position that is evident in *Hind Swaraj*.

---

[54] Ibid., p. 4. With the breakdown of the aristocracy, new forms of government were formed which expressed popular sentiments, thus, allowing a rise in mass consciousness. Social and material changes were affecting concepts of community, and kinships were dissolving (18).

[55] In opposition, there developed Cultural Studies which "negate[d] the specific [elitist] values of [the] Kulturkritiks (xix), and we see this in the works of Walter Benjamin.

[56] Sudipta Kaviraj, "Modernity and Politics in India" *Daedalus* Vol. 129. 1 (Winter, 2000), pp. 137-162. p. 160.

Reading such a text as *Hind Swaraj*, written at the interstices of the moments when the modern Indian nation state was being formulated, allows us, in retrospect, to look at the tensions that were evident when western socio-political changes were introduced and institutionalized within a nation; the coerced march to modernity was not without its contradictory pulls and supposedly regressive pushes into tradition. But in historiographical accounts that narrate about the nation-state, these contradictory elements are often elided. For Dipesh Chakrabarty, as a historian, it is important to be able to write "into the history of modernity the ambivalences, contradictions, the use of force, and the tragedies and ironies that attend it."[57] As he writes,

> What effectively is played down ... in histories that either implicitly or explicitly celebrate the advent of the modern state and the idea of citizenship is the repression and violence that are instrumental in the victory of the modern as is the persuasive power of its rhetorical strategies.[58]

Hind Swaraj is an intervention in any grand narrative we make about the modernization of India and the formation of a nation-state, for the narrative reminds us that this process took place through the constant erasure and elision of its contradictory moves.

For Gandhi, the characteristics of a modern nation were not necessarily beneficial to the people, and the institutions which were considered to be intrinsic to a modern society come under strong criticism in *Hind Swaraj*. The Parliamentary system of government,

---

[57] Dipesh Chakrabarty, "Postcoloniality and the Artifice of History: Who Speaks for 'Indian' Pasts?" in *Provincializing Europe: Postcolonial Thought and Historical Difference* (Princeton, Princeton University Press, 2000), p. 43.

[58] Ibid., pp. 44-45.

where there was a "popular representation,"[59] Gandhi wrote, was problematic as often the individuals involved were more concerned about themselves than about the people whom they represented. The legal system also comes under critique, and he writes, "Do you think that it would be possible for the English to carry on their government without law courts."[60] That British presence and rule was enabled through and because of the legal system is reason enough for the justice system, in its entirety, to be written off. We are made aware of the numerous methods of surveillance that the state uses to control and deprive its members of freedom.

Not surprisingly, *Hind Swaraj* often reads as a piecemeal critique of all the different aspects of modernity – the steam engines, the use of print, trains, automatization, use of machinery, artillery, factories, medicine.[61] Mechanization allows us with spare time, but modern civilization does not address issues of a non-material aspect that would provide one with means to utilize extra time; though industrialization increased efficiency and increased leisure time, it was important to have a moral principle which would guide how humans would "live, spend their free time, and relate to one another"; but as modern society was propelled by the "search for profit," consumerism was the only available option.[62] Gandhi's concern, thus, was with certain psychical conditions, which were not addressed by the advocates of modernity. Civilization, Gandhi proposed, was that "mode of conduct which points out to man the path of duty,"[63] and

---

[59] *Hind Swaraj*, p. 31.

[60] Ibid., p. 61.

[61] Ibid., pp. 36-37.

[62] Bhikhu Parekh, *Gandhi: A very short Introduction* (Oxford: Oxford University Press, 1997), pp. 64-65.

[63] *Hind Swaraj*, p. 67.

could not be quantified by mechanical and industrial advancement. Moreover, the rationalistic attitude of modernity valued only one form of life, "the secular, individualistic, and competitive," negating the possibility of a pluralistic society and tolerance.[64]

Conscious that nationalist leaders were engaging with western discourses of the nation, Gandhi writes that such a concept of the nation was akin to desiring "English rule without the Englishman."[65] He wrote:

> You want the tiger's nature, but not the tiger; that is to say, you would make India English, and, when it becomes English, it will be called not Hindustan but Englistan. This is not the *Swaraj* [freedom] I want.[66]

For most scholars, what is not debatable is that the public sphere of politics was constructed on western models. When Partha Chatterjee attempts to redefine how nationalist thought in postcolonial nations need not necessarily have to be considered as derivative nationalisms, he distinguishes between nationalism as a political movement and nationalism as a cultural construct.[67] In the private domain of culture – that is, the family, religion and customs – the "nation [was] already sovereign, even when the state [was] in the hands of the colonial powers."[68] Gandhi, on the other hand, is involved, at least discursively, in not only forwarding a nationalist agenda which would

---

[64] Parekh, *Gandhi*, p. 68.

[65] *Hind Swaraj*, p. 28.

[66] Ibid, p. 28.

[67] Partha Chatterjee, *The Nation and its Fragments* (Princeton, NJ: Princeton University Press, 1993).

[68] Ibid., p. 191.

emerge from within India, but also in defending the fact that India as a nation was always already imagined into being. "We," he wrote, were "one nation before they [the Britishers] came to India."[69] Religion played an important function in enabling mobility, as pilgrimages all across India compelled people to travel, as "holy places [were] established in various parts of India."[70] In the post-Mughal period, foreigners were able to blend within the nation as India had and has a "faculty of assimilation."[71] The introduction of foreigners did not necessarily destroy the nation; "those who are conscious of the spirit of nationality do not interfere with one another's religion."[72] Conscious of the fact that communalism was a result of British presence and their policy of divide and rule, Gandhi's assessment comes across as a harsh reminder that historically, religion could not define national affiliation, as often historically, Moslems and the Hindus share the same ancestors.[73] The civilization that Gandhi wanted was "synthetic" and "tolerant" and he rarely uses the term nation and when doing so, he meant *swadeshi*, i.e., a "love of one's country."[74]

It is easy to write off Gandhi as an aberration, resisting against the inevitable. But it is important to remember that though Gandhi was writing a hundred years ago, trying to theorize about certain aspects

---

[69] *Hind Swaraj*, p. 48.

[70] Ibid, p. 49.

[71] Ibid., p. 52.

[72] Ibid., p. 52.

[73] Ibid., p. 53.

[74] Bhikhu Parekh, *Gandhi's Political Philosophy* (Notre Dame: University of Notre Dame, 1989), pp. 193-194.

of a non-modern society in his vision of how a nation could become, his central attempt was to grasp on to those characteristics of a traditional society before they disappeared forever. Not only was he resisting colonial rule, but he, along with Nehru and Tagore, though differently, were negotiating with modernity in articulating a vision of a post-British India. To what extent can tradition – if this connotes pre-British India – co-exist alongside modernity? Is tradition a mere adherence of what was a "mere collection of precedents," or is it a "form of inquiry," binding as it has "survived the rigorous test of lived experience" but not static as every tradition contains an "internal principle of self-criticism."[75] It does us good to remind ourselves that the use of *satyagraha* or non-violence was the means used to disrupt British rule – and successfully so; the strict modes of control and state brutality were counter effected by Gandhi's refusal to conform to methods of conventional war fare. He wrote, "Brute force is not natural to the Indian soil. You will have, therefore, to rely wholly on soul-force. You must not consider that violence is necessary at any stage for reaching our goal."[76] The circuitous route to *satyagraha* incorporated American philosophers like Thoreau and though the result, apparently, indigenous to "Indian soil," cannot solely be contained within one national identity.

---

[75] Ibid., p. 24-25.

[76] *Hind Swaraj*, p. 112.

6 CONCLUSION: THE NEED TO READ PRIMARY TEXTS.

We should broaden our perspective on what we consider as primary sources. Reading from a wide range of texts that were written during the time period of European colonial presence will allow us to arrive at a more sophisticated understanding of how two disparate cultures, of the Center and the metropole, engaged with each other. The following is an example from one of the early newspapers that were printed in Calcutta.

Calcutta Chronicle

Tuesday; August 27th, 1793. Volume VIII.

East India Trade; Liverpool. Nov. 23; 1792.

I. That PEACE is the natural, and ought to be the inseparable attendant of Commerce; that the possession of Continental Territories is valuable only as it is productive of commercial intercourse; and that it is probable the opening of the East India Trade will render less frequent those desolating wars which have so often deluged the soil of that unhappy Country with the blood of its inhabitants, whilst they have been equally fatal to this Country, by the sacrifice of thousands of British subjects, and the expenditure of millions of British treasure.

II. That the East India Monopoly prevents the free export of our manufactures to one of the largest and richest regions of the World, where there is reason to believe they might, in the course of open Trade, be increased in their most twenty fold and upwards: -- that under the present system, the exports are conducted without a proper attention to the change of circumstances and reasons; and due means are not employed for opening new sources of Traffic on the Eastern coast of Africa, the island of Madagascar, the countries that lie up the Straits of Babelmandal, and on the shores of the Persian Gulf, with many of the vast profusion of Islands that are scattered throughout the Indian Ocean, all within the limits of the Company's Monopoly, and yielding them little or no advantage; but which the unfettered enterprise and skill of individuals might soon explore and render of the utmost importance.

III. That this Monopoly cloaks many of the infant Manufacturers of Britain as they arise, from the power it gives of lowering, at pleasure, the rival Manufactures of India in the Home Market; the loss sustained being laid on such articles as are the produce of the soil of India, which habit has rendered necessary amongst us, and which are not to be obtained elsewhere, a power that more than once has destroyed the manufacture of British Porcelain, and that has employed to oppose and bear down the manufacture of Cotton, now risen to such national importance.

www.ingramcontent.com/pod-product-compliance
Lightning Source LLC
Chambersburg PA
CBHW061301040426
42444CB00010B/2458